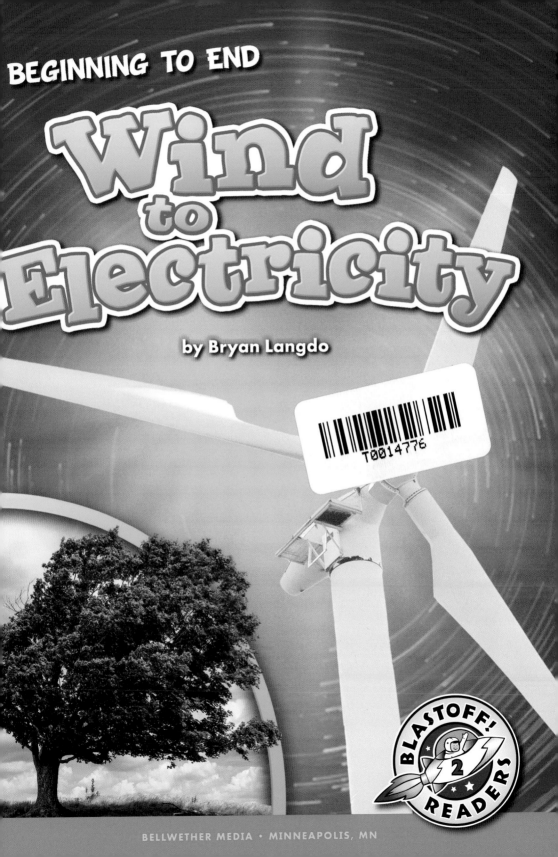

BEGINNING TO END

Wind to Electricity

by Bryan Langdo

BLASTOFF! READERS
2

BELLWETHER MEDIA · MINNEAPOLIS, MN

Blastoff! Readers are carefully developed by literacy experts to build reading stamina and move students toward fluency by combining standards-based content with developmentally appropriate text.

 Level 1 provides the most support through repetition of high-frequency words, light text, predictable sentence patterns, and strong visual support.

 Level 2 offers early readers a bit more challenge through varied sentences, increased text load, and text-supportive special features.

 Level 3 advances early-fluent readers toward fluency through increased text load, less reliance on photos, advancing concepts, longer sentences, and more complex special features.

★ **Blastoff! Universe**

Reading Level

Blastoff! Beginners — Grade **K**

Blastoff! READERS — Grades **1–3**

Blastoff! DISCOVERY — Grade **4**

This edition first published in 2024 by Bellwether Media, Inc.

No part of this publication may be reproduced in whole or in part without written permission of the publisher. For information regarding permission, write to Bellwether Media, Inc., Attention: Permissions Department, 6012 Blue Circle Drive, Minnetonka, MN 55343.

Library of Congress Cataloging-in-Publication Data

Names: Langdo, Bryan, author.
Title: Wind to electricity / by Bryan Langdo.
Description: Minneapolis, MN : Bellwether Media, Inc., 2024. | Series: Blastoff! readers. Beginning to end | Includes bibliographical references and index. | Audience: Ages 5-8 | Audience: Grades 2-3 | Summary: "Relevant images match informative text in this introduction to how wind is turned into electricity. Intended for students in kindergarten through third grade"– Provided by publisher.
Identifiers: LCCN 2023006487 (print) | LCCN 2023006488 (ebook) | ISBN 9798886874273 (library binding) | ISBN 9798886875379 (paperback) | ISBN 9798886876154 (ebook)
Subjects: LCSH: Wind power–Juvenile literature. | Wind power plants–Juvenile literature.
Classification: LCC TJ820 .L3555 2024 (print) | LCC TJ820 (ebook) | DDC 621.31/2136–dc23/eng/20230224
LC record available at https://lccn.loc.gov/2023006487
LC ebook record available at https://lccn.loc.gov/2023006488

Editor: Elizabeth Neuenfeldt   Designer: Laura Sowers

Printed in the United States of America, North Mankato, MN.

Table of Contents

Wind Energy

Electricity is a type of **energy**. It powers phones and lamps. But where does it come from?

Who Makes the Most Wind Energy?

More than a quarter of all wind energy is made in China

Electricity comes from many things. Some electricity comes from wind!

Warm and Cool Air

Wind starts with the sun.
The sun heats the earth.

Air over land heats faster than air over water.

The warm air rises.
Cooler air rushes in
to replace it.

This cool air is wind.
Wind has a lot
of energy!

Blown Away

The highest recorded
wind speed on Earth
was 253 miles
(407 kilometers)
per hour!

At the Wind Farm

wind farm

Wind farms catch
the wind's energy.

Wind farms are in windy places.
Some are in big fields.
Others are in the sea!

Wind farms have tall **turbines**. Each turbine has a **rotor**.

blade →

rotor

turbines

Wind moves across the rotor's blades. The wind's **pressure** pushes the blades. The rotor spins!

generator

The rotor is connected to **gears** and a **generator**. They are inside the turbine.

Parts of the Process

rotor

gears

generator

As the rotor spins,
the generator spins, too.
The spinning generator
makes electricity!

The electricity flows
through **cables**.
It goes to
a **substation**.

The substation makes
the electricity safe
for people to use.

cables

substation

Most of the electricity leaves the substation. Cables carry it across the **power grid**. The power grid brings electricity to homes and businesses.

Wind to Electricity

1 warm air rises, and cool air blows in to make wind

2 wind blows through a wind farm

3 wind turns a turbine's rotor

4 the generator spins to make electricity

5 electricity flows through cables to a substation

6 the electricity is sent for people to use

Renewable Energy

Many people get their electricity from wind. Wind is a kind of **renewable energy**.

We will never run out of it!

Glossary

cables—bundles of wires that carry electricity

energy—power that can be used to do something

gears—wheels with teeth that turn machines

generator—a machine that turns energy into electricity

power grid—a network of wires that deliver electricity

pressure—a force that pushes against something

renewable energy—energy that comes from something that does not run out

rotor—a part of a machine that turns

substation—a place where electricity is changed to make it safe for people to use

turbines—engines that move when air or water flows through them

wind farms—places that have wind turbines to make electricity

To Learn More

AT THE LIBRARY

Carlson Berne, Emma. *Green Energy.* New York, N.Y.: Starry Forest Books, 2021.

Clark, Stacy. *Planet Power: Explore the World's Renewable Energy.* Concord, Mass.: Barefoot Books, 2021.

Mikoley, Kate. *How Do Wind Turbines Work?* New York, N.Y.: PowerKids Press, 2021.

ON THE WEB

FACTSURFER

Factsurfer.com gives you a safe, fun way to find more information.

1. Go to www.factsurfer.com.

2. Enter "wind to electricity" into the search box and click 🔍.

3. Select your book cover to see a list of related web sites.

Index

The images in this book are reproduced through the courtesy of: Bennyartist, front cover; SixMillionMangos, front cover (inset); Wichai Prasomsri1, p. 3; kali9, pp. 4-5; Styve Reineck, p. 6; ESB Professional, pp. 6-7; underworld, p. 8; Rainer Fuhrmann, pp. 8-9; Altitude Drone, p. 10; Tom Buysse, pp. 10-11; arrogant, pp. 12-13 (turbine), 23; mirounga, pp. 12-13, 19 (3); Stephen Barnes/Energy/ Alamy, pp. 14-15, 19 (4); engel.ac, p. 15 (rotor); BjÃ¶rn Bartsch, p. 15 (gears); Mark Boulton/ Alamy, p. 15 (generator); Blue Planet Studio, pp. 16, 19 (2, 5); StockPhotosArt, pp. 16-17; Jose Luis Stephens, p. 18; Anton Gvozdikov, p. 19 (1); Justin_Krug, p. 19 (6); Chun han, pp. 20-21; Lordn, p. 21.